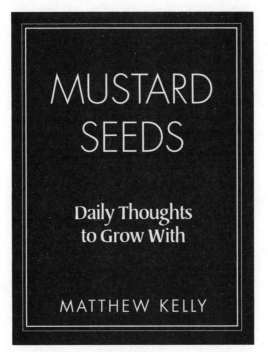

MUSTARD SEEDS

Daily Thoughts to Grow With

M A T T H E W   K E L L Y

Mustard Seeds
Daily Thoughts to Grow With

ISBN: 978-1-929266-04-3

Library of Congress Cataloging–in Publication Data

The Best Version of Yourself® and
Dynamic Catholic® and Be Bold. Be Catholic.®
are registered trademarks of
The Dynamic Catholic Institute.

For more information on this title and
other books and CDs available through the
Dynamic Catholic Book Program, please visit:
www.DynamicCatholic.com

The Dynamic Catholic Institute
2200 Arbor Tech Drive
Hebron, KY 41048
Phone 1–859–980–7900
www.DynamicCatholic.com
Email: info@DynamicCatholic.com

Printed in the United States of America.

⫸ Contents ⫷

I would like to dedicate this book to
Brian Brouggy,
who challenged me to think
and taught me to reason.

⋙ Foreword ⋘

Visiting a friend in Minneapolis last year, I came upon a restless night. As everyone else in the house enjoyed a peaceful sleep, I made my way to the kitchen and looked for something to read. Amid a pile of books I found *A Call to Joy*. The author was a young man named Matthew Kelly. Looking at his twenty-four year old face, I cracked the cover with understandable reluctance. What, I wondered, could this "kid" know about life, about true joy or about God? Quite a lot, actually.

Four years ago, a typical teenager from Australia and one of eight brothers, Matthew Kelly heard what he believes to be the voice of God. Nothing in his background or in his religious upbringing would suggest that he was meant for such an experience. In the last few years, Matthew has traveled the world to share the messages he believes emanate from a divine source.

When I finished the book, I realized that I'd stumbled onto something or someone with a life-changing message. Wanting to share what I'd learned, I invited Matthew Kelly on to my television show. And even though his written message touched me deeply, I admit I met him as a skeptic. His truth, his insight, and the directness of his approach seemed too clear, too accessible and too easy.

Many people presume that if God speaks to us, the message will be dramatic and overwhelming. We've come to expect that true prophets will be filled with hellfire, brimstone and tales of future cataclysm. Not Matthew Kelly. His messages assure, counsel, challenge, empower and give delightful insight into the gentle goodness of a God who is truly for us.

Professionally religious people seem universally surprised at and delighted by this young adult with a message. Father Dan O'Connell, a Jesuit who once served as President of St. Louis University, said: "After listening to Matthew, I felt like telling the whole world to tune into him. His words are those of Christ. He is truly on a mission from the Father." The popular writer Father Joseph Girzone, whose own book *Joshua* touched millions, says of Matthew Kelly: "His heart and mind have been touched by God. It is the only way I can explain the beauty and depth of his thoughts."

It would be a mistake to cast Matthew Kelly in the role of a strange mystic who gets radio signals from above. His messages are real and significant. But they are not unlike the messages any one of us gets when we work to communicate with or listen to the Lord.

Maybe Matthew's real gift is his ability to convey the beauty and depth of God's friendship. Most of us, I suspect, would have difficulty recounting the ways in which God speaks to us.

We know He's there, we feel his presence, but it's an intimacy of experience in which words often fail. With Matthew Kelly, they don't. More than a message giver, Matthew is like an interpreter for the soul, helping us to say and express what we know and feel but can't always articulate. He has a real gift.

Since our initial interview, I've spoken often with Matthew Kelly. I never cease to be amazed by the youthful and valued zeal he feels for the things of God. And for a church which has the truth, but not always the means for communicating that truth effectively, he is a breath of fresh and vibrant air.

Many of us know that a relationship with the Lord and a focus on ideas which matter are passions strongly to be desired. But in the hurly burly of daily life, it's not always easy to center ourselves. Work and school, family and friends, the need of sleep and for exercise, the necessity of eating and paying our bills, all conspire to keep us from pinpointing the heart of life's meaning. Enter Matthew Kelly's wonderful new book, *Mustard Seeds*. The short, centered, meaningful, thought-provoking, and God-aligning words of this book are a special gift and grace for us all. Like the "grabbed air" we take in to swim a little farther, Matthew's words fuel the heart, the mind and the soul. This book is grace.

MONSIGNOR JIM LISANTE

Introduction

I was born and raised in Australia and so far life has been a rich and exciting experience for me.

If I were to dedicate the rest of my life to writing I would not be able to sufficiently expand on the ideas in this volume. It seems today that everything in our lives we do quickly. Try to ponder this book slowly.

In each of these brief passages I have tried to present a seed of truth. Sow the seed in the rich and fertile soil of your heart. Water it with the flowing waters of contemplation and allow the sunlight of life's experiences to shine upon it. The seed will grow into a wonderful tree bearing the fruits of: peace, joy, humility, integrity, wisdom, and love.

In the last five years of my life there has been no shortage of moments in which to reflect and no shortage of experiences to reflect upon. At various times particular thoughts have struck me, and so, I have written them down. I know I am not the first to write about some of these ideas. Nonetheless, I believe all of them to be true and have found them useful in my struggle to grow spiritually. The truth in some of them does not scream out at you. Do not consider something false or worthless just because its truth is not immediately evident.

What fills the pages of this book I wrote primarily for myself. I now share these seeds with you because I know how they have helped me.

These words will challenge you to think, reflect, ponder, and pray. This book will help you to see the person you are and the person you can be. Open your heart and mind, and your life will change gracefully.

MATTHEW KELLY

⊰ January 1 ⊱

You are always worrying about all the things you are not.
What about all the things you are?

⊰ January 2 ⊱

To be busy opposing wrong is not the same as being right.

⊰ January 3 ⊱

Suppose I gave you the next five minutes to decide what you
want to do for the next twenty-four hours. Now, let us make
the assumption that you will live on earth for about seventy-
five years. That seventy-five years compared to eternity is like
the five minutes you take to plan your day.

January 4

It is my belief that in every person there is an innate goodness.
Seek it out and help it to grow.

January 5

Some people look at the wonderful and beautiful things of this
world and say to themselves, "I must have these things."
Others admire the splendor, wonder, and beauty of the things
of this world and wonder, "How much greater the things of
God must be." The latter is a small group and you should
strive to be numbered among them.

January 6

Next time someone asks you to pray for them, pray for them.

January 7

The world discourages. God encourages.

January 8

To be a leader of people sometimes you have to
turn your back on them.

January 9

Water runs downhill and so do human beings.
So will you spiritually if you don't make an effort.

January 10

So many people have a conversion and lose their profession.
God sends His laborers into the world to re-Christianize
every environment and every honest human activity.

January 11

You can learn more in an hour of silence
than you can in a year from books.

January 12

For God time is the unfolding of truth that already is,
the unveiling of beauty that is yet to be.

January 13

There is a difference between discretion and fear. There is a
difference between prudence and fear. There is a difference
between discernment and fear. Fear is not a virtue.

January 14

You don't have to open your mouth to pray.

January 15

If you want to be wise, get to know yourself. After a knowledge
of God there is no greater practical wisdom than knowledge of
self. And from this self-knowledge will flow the children of
wisdom: humility, prudence, and discretion.

January 16

Don't interpret another person's kindness as weakness.

January 17

To be sincere is to let people get to know
the real person you are.

January 18

Are you allowing God to use you as an instrument?
Or, are you using God?

January 19

Common sense is not so common. Develop an awareness
of the needs of those around you and common sense
and you will be a leader.

January 20

You cannot become more like Christ and stay as you are.

January 21

Develop the ability to give people: a healing look,
a healing word, or, a healing touch.

January 22

God's plea to humanity has always been a call to go within
and discover the truth about ourselves, which is that we
have been created in the image and likeness of God.
Our relationship with God begins to blossom when we go
within and discover the rich, beautiful, and complex
creations that we are individually and uniquely.
This call to go within, prayer, and indeed, the sacraments,
are designed to lead us to our fulfillment. It is this fulfillment
that brings us joy and happiness, which is the will of God,
and which also brings most glory to God.

January 23

So many people in the world do not know Jesus. Of those that do know Him, many know His name, few know His ways.

January 24

Each night before you go to bed think about the most positive thing that happened to you that day. If you are married share it with your spouse and ask them to share with you the most positive experience of their day.

January 25

"The eyes are not satisfied with seeing." Mortify your senses for children of God should live holy purity and the eyes are the windows to the soul.

January 26

Go for long walks in quiet places.

January 27

Human labor alone cannot achieve a divine purpose.

January 28

There is a lot of talk, it seems, about the second coming.
When will Jesus come again? The Lord will not be late in
coming; He will not come early. He will come at the same time
He came the first time. He will come "in the fullness of time."
He will come at the most appropriate time,
for that is the fullness of time.

January 29

You learn more from your friends than you will ever learn
from books. Choose your friends wisely.

January 30

You are in debt to all because God has given you many gifts, the
fruits of which He intended for you to share
with all those that cross your path.

January 31

Examine your conscience daily. Have I prayed today?
Did I struggle to avoid distractions in my prayer?
How have I offended God? Have I been: envious, proud, lazy,
gluttonous, lustful, angry, covetous? Have I cared for my family?
Have I prayed for them? Have I assisted them in whatever way I
can with the temporal necessities? Have I helped my friends?
Did I do my work well? How can I do it better?
Did I waste time?
Then make a resolution to change and an act of contrition.

February 1

Each Friday at 3p.m. spend one minute thinking about the suffering involved in being crucified.

February 2

When Jesus was on the cross He didn't turn to the man next to Him and say, "You committed the crime, pay the price." No, He offered him a better life.

February 3

Have you ever known the joy of receiving an unexpected letter? Wonderful isn't it? Write a letter today. The apostolate of letter writing is a powerful one.

February 4

Jesus Christ: true God, true man, and, true friend.

February 5

If relations between you and someone dear to you have grown cold and distant, warm their heart again by saying to that person "I love you" at the end of each day or conversation.

February 6

Remember, when things get tough just take it one day at a time, praying and working. When things get really tough just take it one hour at a time, being friendly to those around you and doing what you have to do. And when things get really, really, tough, just take life moment by moment.
Do the best you can and leave the rest to Our Lord.
We have to give Him our "five loaves and two fishes."
Then He will work the miracle and feed the "five thousand."
Grace builds on nature and so we have to do our bit.

February 7

Personal holiness is the answer to every problem.

February 8

Somewhere deep inside you know that generous love
is the answer and the only road.

February 9

When two people love each other it is a wonderful thing,
but when two people love God and each other this is the kind
of relationship from which the future of the Church will spring.
When you both burn with a love of God the fire will consume
the impurities of your human love. The more you love God
the more you will be able to love each other.

February 10

When you are advising people don't tell them
the negative things they shouldn't do, tell them the
positive things they should do.

February 11

There is nothing more attractive than holiness.

February 12

Without humility there is no virtue. Humility is
the foundation of all the other virtues.

February 13

Regardless of the best plan you can put together for yourself
with the greatest of your imagination, God has something
much greater planned. If only you will surrender.

February 14

To be loved you must love.

February 15

Pray for vocations, yes, but pray also that you can live
your vocation more fully.

February 16

Treat the people you live with as if today is the last day
you have to spend with them. One day you will be right
and you will be glad you did.

February 17

Grace brings light to the mind, power to the will,
and love to the heart.

February 18

Don't fight, avoid, destroy, or resent silence. Does silence have
a feeling of emptiness? Don't resist. Learn to relax in silence and
let God's love fill you. The fullness of love is in silence.

February 19

Ask your Guardian Angel. Your request will be granted unless it is sinful or runs against the will of God.

February 20

It is not enough for us to avoid sin. We must grow in virtue. Mortification is the foundation of all virtue.

February 21

You think you are perfect. You are not. You are imperfect, but perfectible.

February 22

Today send someone a copy of a good spiritual book.

February 23

There is a time to speak and a time to listen.
A child of God must know the difference.

February 24

Very often the slightest circumstances change
the direction of our lives.

February 25

Your fears are bad counsellors.

February 26

People gather together in groups for good and bad reasons.
Even when the reason is good the effect on an individual
can be bad.

February 27

You must learn to love with detachment. Love to love,
not to be loved.

February 28

When you know you are doing the will of God, that alone
is enough to sustain your happiness. When you don't have
that, all the possessions in the world cannot sustain happiness
in the depths of your heart.

───────────────── ⤐ March 1 ⇜ ─────────────────

Young people look forward. Old people look backward. If you always take time to look forward, you will remain young.

───────────────── ⤐ March 2 ⇜ ─────────────────

If you want to be happy, if you want to be calm and peaceful, if you want your life to be filled with joy: pray. Peace, joy, and happiness are the fruits of silent prayer.

───────────────── ⤐ March 3 ⇜ ─────────────────

God is only as far away as we place Him and never as far away as we think. For it is in Him that we live, move, and have our being.

March 4

You talk too much.

March 5

Hold your right hand in front of you and visualize one person on
each finger — people you can help grow closer to God.
Pray each day for these people. Try to develop your friendship
with each of them by spending time with them individually.
See them at least once a month on a one-to-one basis.
Show an active interest in their interests. Do not mention God
or religion unless they introduce these topics
to your conversation.
If they do introduce the topics comment only briefly.
After twelve months you will have built a friendship based on
selflessness that demands respect. This friendship will then
become the vehicle for the truth to spread.

March 6

If you pray, God will lead you. If you follow, He will reward you.

March 7

The road less travelled is the road to salvation.

March 8

The secret to lasting success is knowing where
your gifts come from.

March 9

One of the most worthy sentiments of the human heart
is hope, a tendency towards something morally good
and in itself human.
Our sustenance in the midst of difficulties and obstacles,
encountered in the struggle to attain perfection, is the virtue
of supernatural hope. The object of this hope is eternal life.

March 10

Trust. Surrender. Believe. Receive.

March 11

Learn to be content.

March 12

Jesus said, "Peace I give you, my peace I leave you."
He gave it to you, have you lost it? Go to Him today
and ask Him to fill you with peace.

March 13

So many of our churches are closed all day long.
When asked, "Why?" the most common reason given is
vandalism. If each of us spent fifteen minutes a day in our
churches there would always be a steady flow of people
through our churches. If we are in our churches they won't
close our churches. If we are in our churches they won't
vandalize our churches.

March 14

When was the last time you spoke a kind word of
encouragement to somebody? Speak one today.

March 15

I cannot imagine Jesus by Joseph's side in the workshop in
Nazareth being lazy. I can imagine Jesus working hard and
well, and paying attention to the details of His work. Isn't that
how you should work?

March 16

There are endless possibilities for practicing mortification.

March 17

Our lives are journeys seeking truth. Pilate asked,
"What is truth?" Jesus told us in the gospels, "I am the Way,
the Truth, and the Life." And somewhere within you,
you know, "The truth will set you free."

March 18

For those that love God there is only victory
and victory for eternity.

March 19

Too many people would have you believe that the perfume of God
is pain and suffering. It is not. God's perfume is happiness.

March 20

You asked me to suggest a book for you to read. Read these:
Matthew, Mark, Luke, and John. Then, when you are finished,
read them again.

March 21

Society breeds an attitude that to be busy is important, and so,
you think your job is to keep busy. Rather, the task before you
each day is to maintain a steady pace and to keep from being
so busy that the voice of God in your life is drowned.

March 22

You are master to others and a slave to yourself. A Christian must be master of self and slave to others.

March 23

You are a human being. You have a body and a soul. The two are inseparable until death. The body, as we know it now, is temporal, but the soul is eternal. What is eternal should lead and reign over that which is temporal.

March 24

When you allow your soul to be saturated with grace through prayer, the sacraments, and a constant effort to remain united to God throughout the day, then you will begin to live your ordinary life divinely.

March 25

Souls are won for Christ only by the sufferings of others.

March 26

Tell children the truth.
They know when you are lying.

March 27

Go out of your way to encourage young people.

March 28

God is slow to anger and full of love. You seem quick to anger
and so the depth of your love is in question.

March 29

Before you open your mouth to criticize, to slander,
remember it is easy to destroy a person's reputation.
You never know the effect of the words you utter in a
thoughtless moment. You never know the damage.
The greater the damage the greater your debt.

We have built into us a desire to be like God
and yet we cannot be God. It is the friction
caused by these two facts that leads us to sin.
Very often we choose the "apparent good" and "eat the fruit"
believing that this will lead us to independence and
to become like God. Very often we choose the
"apparent good" believing that such is a valid response
to the desire within us to be like God. It is not.
We cross the line of valid response to the desire to be like
God when we forget, conveniently or otherwise,
that we are dependent, and always will be dependent,
on God for our existence.
When we seek independence from God, we seek and find
catastrophe, disaster, darkness, useless suffering, despair
and anxiety.
For us to be independent of God is impossible yet we continue
to seek it. The first sign is always disobedience,
or infidelity to the Word of God.

Find something good in each person you meet
and help it to grow.

————————— ❧ April 1 ❦ —————————

When I say, "everything is going to be all right," I don't mean
that everything is going to be as you want it to be.

————————— ❧ April 2 ❦ —————————

Time directs, heals, teaches, and leads hearts to love.
Be patient with yourself and with others. Be patient with God.

————————— ❧ April 3 ❦ —————————

Try to connect or link the new things you are learning
to those you already know. This way you will learn
much more effectively.

⊰ April 4 ⊱

Your character is your destiny.

⊰ April 5 ⊱

Look at a single red rose. Contemplate its beauty and complexity as part of God's creation. When you can appreciate the wonder of this rose, how much more you will appreciate the next person you meet as a wonder of God's creation.

⊰ April 6 ⊱

Lack of punctuality is a disregard for the value of another person's time, and thus, a lack of charity.

⊰ April 7 ⊱

God bestows His wisdom upon men and women in the classroom of silence. May silence become a great friend of yours.

April 8

Sometimes you need to hold on
and sometimes you need to let go.
Ask God to show you which is in His plan for you now.

April 9

Do you remember the cry of Bartimaeus the blind man,
"Jesus son of David have pity on me." This was the first time
in the gospels that Jesus was recognized
as the prophesied son of David.
If you need to be healed emotionally, physically, or spiritually,
I challenge you to cry out to Jesus in faith
and ask Him to heal you.

April 10

In this age when people think they have gained freedom
the tyrant is mediocrity.

April 11

Exercise at least twice a week.

April 12

We all share at least one thing in common. Every man and every woman yearns for happiness. Your yearning for happiness is a yearning for God. Only God can satisfy the yearning for happiness that comes from the very depths of your being.

April 13

Just because someone has their eyes closed does not mean they are asleep. Just because someone has their eyes open does not mean they can see.

April 14

Men and women are unique but equal. It seems the modern western world is unable to comprehend this profound truth.

ᴈ April 15 ᴇ

We all live lives of contemplation. The question is what do you contemplate? Is it the riches of the world, or women walking by in the street? Is it fame and power? Or, is it the wonders of God, His creation, and His spiritual gifts to humanity?

ᴈ April 16 ᴇ

I saw a lady walking in her garden. Then the phone began to ring inside her house. She carried on regardless.
Free yourself from the slavery of modern technology.

ᴈ April 17 ᴇ

Hard work is good for the soul.

ᴈ April 18 ᴇ

At times a fraud can seem like the real thing, but the real thing does not seem like a fraud.

April 19

Within you there is a hidden potential to be great.
Everybody can be great because everybody can serve.

April 20

You seem intent on taking the easy road and I have tried
over and over to gently persuade you not to. Let me tell you
plainly and clearly. The easy road does not lead to heaven
and there are only two eternal destinations.

April 21

"I am a sinner." Reach this awareness. Make this confession;
it is the first condition for salvation.

April 22

If you sow thistles you will not reap corn.

⇥ April 23 ⇤

I am nothing. I know nothing. I can do nothing,
but God is everything and He has made Himself mine.

⇥ April 24 ⇤

Some people are considered wise because of what they know,
others are considered wise because of what they live.

⇥ April 25 ⇤

You have fooled yourself into believing that everyone enjoys
your company. The truth is some things you say and do really
irritate the people around you. Think before you speak or act.

⇥ April 26 ⇤

Many people proclaiming errors today sincerely believe that they
are doing the right thing, unfortunately they are sincerely wrong.
The common error these people commit is that
they trust themselves too much.

April 27

How does a pagan live? How does a child of God live?
How do you live?

April 28

Develop the ability to say everything without saying anything.
Action is the loudest voice.

April 29

Next time you see a mother with a child in a carriage
struggling up a flight of stairs, help her.

April 30

The goodness of God is unending and He will never be
outdone in His generosity. Give all you can. He will give more.

⇥ May 1 ↤

God does not change, but I hope you do.

⇥ May 2 ↤

Do you want to solve that problem? Face your problem.
Accept responsibility for your response to the problem.
Forgive everyone in your problem. Then, come to the Lord
and ask Him to heal you.

⇥ May 3 ↤

Look how silly your reasoning is. You can't change everything
so you don't change anything. You can't do everything
so you don't do anything.

❧ May 4 ❧

The liberty and equality that men and women have struggled with and searched for throughout history have been revealed through a simple prayer, the 'Our Father.' If only we could understand and grasp the fact that we are all children of God.

❧ May 5 ❧

Did you eat today? Did you pray today? You fed your body, you must also feed your precious immortal soul.

❧ May 6 ❧

A boy takes a girl from the dance floor not to deny her her other friends, but so that he can communicate with her a little more. Jesus wants to do the same.

❧ May 7 ❧

In the quietness, stillness, and darkness of the night, sit and listen to classical music with the one you love.

---------------------------⊰ May 8 ⊱---------------------------

What we do to one another we do to Christ and to ourselves.

---------------------------⊰ May 9 ⊱---------------------------

Treat your girlfriend only in the ways you would
if her mother and father were present.

---------------------------⊰ May 10 ⊱---------------------------

Read the gospels and observe those who live by fear.
Look also at those who trust Jesus and live by faith.
Don't let fear paralyze you. Trust in Jesus.

---------------------------⊰ May 11 ⊱---------------------------

A very dear friend of mine finished one of her letters with this
line: "Help me to remember that when I have God
things will always be in place."
I pray we help each other to remember.

❧ May 12 ❧

Do this for your friends and you will be a true friend:
Teach them to love;
teach them to be loved; and
lead them to God.
Do this for me and you will be a true friend of mine:
Teach me to love;
teach me to be loved; and
lead me to God.

❧ May 13 ❧

Throughout the ages some people have been touched by Christ
and gone out and told the world. Christ wants you to be
numbered among them.

❧ May 14 ❧

There is a difference between the human silence of
embarrassment or shame and the divine silence in which
love finds its rest. You must attain the latter.

May 15

Your defeats in the eyes of the world are so often your victories in the eyes of God.

May 16

Is Jesus the center of your life?

May 17

You don't seem to be at peace? Peace is lost through sin, pride, and insincerity. So go to confession and avoid sin, practice humility, and be sincere with yourself and with God. Then, ask God to grant you peace.

May 18

Personal holiness is the beginning of everything and the answer to everything.

To pray so as to grow and become more like Christ is the
challenge of every Christian. To spread the gospel message of
Christ in its fullness is the mission that accompanies baptism.
The latter demands the former.
You cannot give what you do not have.
God is calling you to turn on the tap of your spiritual life.
Not full blast, but just to a steady drip. If you put a bucket
under a dripping tap eventually it will fill and once it is full it
has to overflow. There is nowhere else for the water to go.
The tap is our interior lives. The drops of water are the peace,
joy, love and happiness that are the fruits of prayer.
The bucket is our hearts and souls.
Drop by drop, through prayer and the sacraments,
we are filled with this peace, joy, love and happiness,
and once full we too will overflow.
It is then that every place we go,
every person we are with, begins to benefit
from the overflowing of this peace, joy, love, and happiness,
that we allow to flow from Christ through our words, actions,
and even by our mere presence.
When we love God, the conversion of society
and the people around us will not have to be premeditated.
It will be natural.

⇥ May 20 ⇤

The world is full of good people. So many people believe,
because of the influence the media has on them, that the world
is full of bad people. In all my travels across the world I have
never met one bad person. Where are all these bad people?
They are in our imaginations and on our television sets.
The world is full of good people.

⇥ May 21 ⇤

In the depths of your heart you still desire a pure love.

⇥ May 22 ⇤

Never install a fear of defeat in a child. A Christian must be
able to respond to times of defeat and thrive again.

⇥ May 23 ⇤

Give some money to support someone else's dream.

⇥ May 24 ⇤

When you are experiencing trials or troubles in your life,
remember everything in life, no matter how bad,
comes to an end.

⇥ May 25 ⇤

If you cannot hate sin you cannot love God.

⇥ May 26 ⇤

You tell me of those that are hungry, those that are oppressed,
and those that are unemployed. Greater than these are the
sufferings of those that are lonely, and greater still are the
sufferings of those that do not know Jesus Christ.
Don't throw up your arms in horror at the world's sufferings,
but roll up your sleeves and do something to alleviate them.

⇥ May 27 ⇤

With people gathering for all sorts of reasons in great crowds society has almost been convinced of the overabundance of people. We have forgotten how to appreciate and reverence the wonderful treasure, the pearl, within each person.

⇥ May 28 ⇤

The "being" of something changeable is not only what it actually is, but what it still can be. Our potential as human beings is enormous, but relatively unexplored.

⇥ May 29 ⇤

Joy is the fruit of appreciation.

⇥ May 30 ⇤

You tell me that you are an atheist. For just a moment assume that God does exist, that He is shaping history, and that He is moving humanity toward some destiny. Wouldn't you like to know about all of that if it really were true?

God is the glue in relationships. If you don't have the glue,
sooner or later the relationship will fall apart.

⟫ June 1 ⟪

If you want to be a man or woman of God you must pray.
If you want to be a man or woman of prayer then you must
make silence a good friend of yours. Silence on the inside and
silence on the outside.
It is in silence that you will align your heart, mind,
and soul with God.

⟫ June 2 ⟪

God rewards every good work.

⟫ June 3 ⟪

I've done enough travelling to know, even at my age,
that the only journey is the inner journey.

─────── ❯❯ June 4 ❮❮ ───────

Take time to establish your desires both for your soul and for your life on this earth. The latter should lead to the attainment of the former, but most people never withdraw from the world long enough to discover what it is they really want.

─────── ❯❯ June 5 ❮❮ ───────

They asked me, "Do you feel you are preaching
to the converted?"
"Show me someone who is converted and you will show me
a person who needs a conversion," I replied.

─────── ❯❯ June 6 ❮❮ ───────

This weekend go and sit in a playground and
watch the children play.

─────── ❯❯ June 7 ❮❮ ───────

Cherish your wife. She is a gift. Love the gift,
but don't love the gift more than the giver.

June 8

Sin is to step out from under the umbrella of God.
It is not so much that God will punish you for it, but that you
have stepped out from under His loving protection.
Separation from God is the worst punishment of all.

June 9

It is not enough to be a nice person.

June 10

You are impatient with people. You are obviously not aware
of the presence of Christ in people. Open your eyes and
see that how you treat that person you treat Christ.

June 11

Morality is not democracy.

June 12

You will never reach perfection unless you determine to make it a goal. Then, if you are to grow at all in human perfection, you must make an effort.

June 13

Your ambition for power has rendered you powerless. Discover the ways in which you seek power and understand the inadequacies of your character that lead you to such behavior. Overcome the need to be in control and you will be set free.

June 14

Truth does not change. Truth is not a variable.
Truth is a constant and the equation is eternity.

June 15

You never hesitate to praise a colleague or a stranger.
Now you must develop the maturity and humility required to praise those close to you, your family and friends.

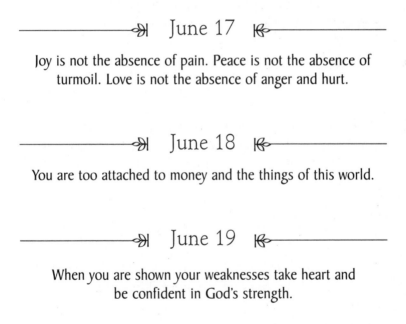

June 16

To all those around you, you seem to be saying nothing because your mouth is not moving. However, God hears the endless chatter of the thoughts in your mind. He hears you judging and condemning those around you.

June 17

Joy is not the absence of pain. Peace is not the absence of turmoil. Love is not the absence of anger and hurt.

June 18

You are too attached to money and the things of this world.

June 19

When you are shown your weaknesses take heart and be confident in God's strength.

⇥ June 20 ⇤

The Father is unlimited joy and He shares that joy with us
when we go into silence, close our eyes and contemplate the
many wonderful gifts He has given us. Too often we only
appreciate them by experiencing the contrast. We get sick;
we appreciate the good health we once had.
Joy and happiness come from appreciating what we have and
who we are with, when we have it and when we are with them.

⇥ June 21 ⇤

Excellence is not greatness. Greatness is the potential of the
unknown lived, and joy is the feeling that accompanies it.
We've lost the magic of unveiling the unknown.

⇥ June 22 ⇤

If you knew more about the saints and how they lived
their lives, you would be more like the saints.

June 23

Your virtue will never be more tested than by your family.

June 24

A friend of mine came up to me the other day and said,
"I'm having trouble fitting God into my life."
God doesn't want to be fitted into our lives. God wants
everything from each one of us, but the reality is you don't give
everything to somebody you don't know.
God calls us to prayer. By praying a little more we will know
Him more; in knowing Him more we will be able to trust Him
more; and in trusting Him more we will be prepared to
abandon ourselves a little more to Him.
PRAY, KNOW, TRUST, ABANDON.

June 25

Don't let the day pass without pondering the angelic civiliza-
tion that surrounds you. They are smarter than you;
call on them for assistance.

June 26

What the Church needs is youth. Youthfulness is not about being young; it is about allowing courage to rule over fear; it's about enthusiasm. When the enthusiasm fades then pessimism begins to set in and people become old.
As Christians our hope sustains our enthusiasm and our youth.

June 27

God speaks to us all in a variety of ways. He speaks to us where we are and in a way we can understand.

June 28

God doesn't ask much of you, just that you co-operate with the grace that He gives you in each moment.

I was hurrying down the street one day in Sydney, virtually running to meet a friend, when a young man approached me. I didn't stop so he walked along with me. It is so common to be approached in the streets these days and asked to buy something, so I immediately wanted to say to him, "not now I'm in a hurry" regardless of his cause.
As he approached me I prepared this answer, but before I could speak he asked me this question, "Do you believe in God?"
I said, "absolutely" but because I had already determined the way the conversation would progress the following was the exchange that resulted.
He said, "Do you believe in God?" I replied, "Absolutely, but not now I'm in a hurry."
Taken literally this wasn't what I meant, but how often in my life these words from my own mouth have summed up my attitude towards God portrayed by my actions.

Satan wants to orphan you. He wants to drag you away from your Father. He wants to steal from you the Spirit that leads you to cry "Abba Father."

———————————— ⇥ July 1 ⇤ ————————————

Our faith is compatible with every honest human activity.
By transforming the activities of our days into prayer we put
God at the center of everything we do. Offer each task of
each day to God as a prayer for a particular intention.

———————————— ⇥ July 2 ⇤ ————————————

Angels are so unemployed these days. Call on the angels today
and everyday; they will not refuse the assistance you need.

———————————— ⇥ July 3 ⇤ ————————————

For a joyful, peaceful, successful relationship you need
spiritual and mental union.

⇥ July 4 ⇤

Independence is an illusion for it denies
our total dependence on God.

⇥ July 5 ⇤

You were telling me about the girl you have just met
and explaining the difficulties you were having with her
because of your beliefs.
On reflection it struck me that she is never going to be more
in love with you than she is now. Anything good and noble
that she won't do for you now, she will never do for you.

⇥ July 6 ⇤

Save 10% of each paycheck you receive. Set it aside in a
separate bank account. You will appreciate the large sum
you will have amassed ten years from today
more than you will miss the 10% now.

July 7

Allow the Spirit to lead you in the moments of the day.

July 8

Nobody knows exactly what they are doing, but if you act like you do people will think you do. Even the greatest leaders will tell you this is true.

July 9

It continues to amaze me everyday that when others come in contact with a person of virtue they comment in awe rather than commenting on a desire to imitate the virtue of that person.

July 10

Is the "gentleman" a dying breed? Maybe not, but certainly an endangered species.

⋙ July 11 ⋘

Why is it so rare to find someone who assures you and
upholds your human dignity?
Are you that person to the people in your life?

⋙ July 12 ⋘

Seldom are we able to help those who are close to us. We
want to help, but we don't know how. We want to give, even of
ourselves, but we don't know which part of ourselves to give.
Nor do we know whether what we have to give is what is
needed. We must learn to let go just as God lets go and
respects the freedom He gave us. Pray and trust.

⋙ July 13 ⋘

You don't ask enough of the right questions. The question you
should be asking is: In what ways can I further imitate Christ
in my daily life?

July 14

It is not enough for us to recognize our nothingness. We must change and become something in the hands of the Lord.

July 15

Our peace is founded not on our perfection but on God's mercy. Call on His mercy.

July 16

What are you? A child of God or a beast?

July 17

David danced for joy before the Ark of the Covenant. John the Baptist danced for joy in the womb of Elizabeth acknowledging the presence of Our Lord. May your life each day be a dance for joy in the presence of the Lord.

⊰ July 18 ⊱

It is through suffering, labor, and death that we enter
into the presence of God.

⊰ July 19 ⊱

Sin is never the answer.

⊰ July 20 ⊱

"This is the will of God: that you be saints"(IThes.4:3).
God wants you to be a saint. If you cannot own this idea
you cannot own heaven.

⊰ July 21 ⊱

You don't have to try some things to know that you don't like
them. You don't have to do some things to know
that they are wrong.

July 22

God provides enough for our need, not our greed.
Give and share.

July 23

You want to know more, but you do not want to live
what you already know.

July 24

Just because there are clouds does not mean
that it is going to rain.

July 25

When I was little if I was travelling on a train with my father
he would hold on to my ticket and would only give it to me
just as I was about to go through the barrier.
Similarly, God will unfold his plans little by little and often
supply your needs only a moment before you require them.

⇥ July 26 ↤

The imbalance that exists in your external activity is a reflection of the imbalance that exists in your heart.

⇥ July 27 ↤

Ask the one whom you love what her hopes and dreams were that got lost along the way while you were too busy thinking about yourself.

⇥ July 28 ↤

Say nothing. You will never regret it.

⇥ July 29 ↤

If you are to resist the ever-present pressures to dilute the Christian ideal of holiness that surround you at every level of society and in almost every environment, you need God's help; you need God's strength; you need God's encouragement. Pray and listen to the voice of God in your life.

July 30

In our lives there comes a time when the only thing that matters is the will of God. For you that time is now.

July 31

Go away alone once a year to a quiet place for a couple of days to pray in silence. Your soul needs rejuvenation. You need a retreat.

August 1

Many of the problems in the world and in the Church
are caused because there are too many self-appointed kings
of nonexistent kingdoms. There is only one Kingdom
and Jesus is the King.

August 2

Only a fool corrects or criticizes someone else
in front of others. Preserve that person's dignity,
take them aside and make your point gently
and with concern for their soul.

August 3

Once you know the purpose of life
everything else falls into place.

⇥ August 4 ⇤

Why is it that you so easily become a victim
of your imagination? Perhaps it is because you allow it
to run loose as a spontaneous response to the smallest matter,
or passing comment, rather than assessing the facts
and maintaining your peace of mind.

⇥ August 5 ⇤

Great men and women are able to make people laugh
and cry and both are a good thing.

⇥ August 6 ⇤

Disappointment is the double edge of the sword of expectation.

⇥ August 7 ⇤

Embrace your God for there is no greater fulfillment in life
than this.

August 8

You cannot love God unfailingly in this life. You can,
however, by cooperating with the grace God grants you,
avoid all deliberate sin.

August 9

If only you would stop ignoring Jesus at your side
in the moments of the day.

August 10

A good teacher explains the lesser known
in terms of the better known.

August 11

It is easier to make a good first impression
than to change a reputation.

August 12

What is holiness? Holiness is an opportunity.
Every person that comes into your life, every circumstance or
event of your life, is an opportunity to be holy.
Your holiness is measured by how lovingly you respond
to God in the moments of the day.
Most of us recognize that we want to love God.
The problem is that we are inconsistent at grasping the
moments of the day one by one for God. If we examine
ourselves individually the reason we will find for our
inconsistent response to God is that our lives of prayer
reflect the same inconsistency.
If we feel like praying we pray and if we don't feel like praying
we don't pray. The problem with this approach is that if we link
our love of God to our selfish feelings, if indeed our love
of God is dictated by our selfish feelings then obviously
there is a contradiction, love being selfless.
God calls you not only to prayer but to consistent prayer.
The more consistency you can bring to your prayer life,
the more consistent your response to God will be
in the moments of the day.

August 13

Take time to reflect on your story — the story of your life.
If not you may lose the thread of your life, your source
of identity, and your purpose.

August 14

There is a freedom that cannot be taken from you.
There is an inner freedom that nobody can ever deny you of,
even if they lock you in a cell and block you off from the
world. Seek that freedom.

August 15

You were made for greater things.

August 16

Maximum effort means minimum risk.

August 17

I think one of the problems in relationships is that people get tired of saying thank you. Very often problems in human relationships reflect problems in our relationship with God. Do you thank people enough? Do you thank God enough?

August 18

It is all right not to have all the answers.

August 19

Trust and understanding of self worth are the two things that lead to happiness and the most basic principles of Christianity. Yet they are the very things we kill.
When someone cannot trust, when someone feels worthless, how can that person be happy?
Your role as an individual in society is to be honest so as to invoke trust, and to compliment and thank others for helping you, or bringing joy to your life, so as to encourage the self esteem of all.
If you want a successful and happy relationship foster an understanding of self worth and be honest.

⇥ August 20 ⇤

There is much confusion during these times regarding
what are and what are not legitimate spiritual practices.
The path of Christian spirituality is well trodden.

⇥ August 21 ⇤

There are enough cowardly people in the world with no
backbone. What is needed are men and women with courage.

⇥ August 22 ⇤

Imagine how difficult things would be if you were blind.
Imagine if you couldn't walk how difficult it would be
to continue the lifestyle you live today.
Don't wait until you are sick to appreciate your health.
Thank the Lord today.

⇥ August 23 ⇤

In prayer you need to open the wounds and clean them and cut
out any disease. You have to be honest with yourself; it hurts,
but the result is your soul will return to better health.

August 24

When you love God, when you truly live your faith,
people will ask, "What makes you different?" Or, "Who or what
inspires you to live the life you live?" People will be attracted
to you and your way of life; they will want what you have. Why?
Christ is attractive and there is nothing more attractive
in a human being than virtue.
When Christ was on the earth people wanted to be with Him.
If He was in the synagogue teaching, or walking down
the street, or eating at someone's house,
whatever He was doing people wanted to be with Him.
When you live the faith people will want to be with you. Why?
It will no longer be you that lives, but Christ that lives in you.

August 25

Have your friends let you down? Have they turned their back
on you? Can you feel the pain of rejection?
Imagine how Jesus felt.

August 26

You came to me discouraged and began telling me about the
problems in the world. Then, in the midst of our conversation
you asked me, "Do you think the world will ever change?"
I replied, "The world will certainly change. The question is,
will it change for the better or for the worse?
The world will change if you and I keep changing.
While you and I keep changing for the worse, the world
will change for the worse. But, when you and I start changing
for the better, the world will change for the better."

August 27

God will take care of you.

August 28

Sometimes people just need you to be with them
in their brokenness.

August 29

When you study put the initials of someone you know who needs prayers at the top of each page. Then offer the work on that page to God as a prayer for that particular person. By doing this you will transform your study into prayer and you will be more aware of God's presence.

August 30

Always be honest with your doctor.

August 31

There comes a time when things seem against you although they really aren't, when you don't feel appreciated although you really are, when the self appointed kings of non-existent kingdoms cause you problems and you don't know where to turn. Turn to Jesus; it is time for another conversion.

September 1

I look around me in my travels everyday to see the wonders of creation: the sun that enlightens, the stars that shine, the moon that glows, the ocean and its creatures, the birds of the sky, the flowers and the trees. Our God created all these, how great He must be. I come to my prayer some days and contemplate the wonders of creation and the fact that all of these are but a dim reflection of the God that created them. So great is God.

September 2

You are only what God allows you to be and nothing more.

September 3

Isn't it time you gave yourself to God completely, once and for all?

September 4

I often wondered as a young person what the secret was
to being a good parent. Reflecting on my childhood
now I can see clearly that my mother and father taught me
with their actions. The secret: be there. Be there
for your children. It is not about quality time;
it's about quantity time.

September 5

Next time you go to a restaurant with people take the worst
seat, the place with the worst view. In doing so you will have
less distractions and will be able to give your attention
more fully to those you are with.

September 6

With patience time will be your friend.

September 7

When the skies are grey and you need inspiration and
motivation ponder the passion and death of Our Lord Jesus.
Then your heart will be inspired to love. Then your heart
will be moved to suffer out of love.

September 8

It is one thing to pray, it is another to live what you discover
in prayer. May God grant you wisdom enough to pray and
strength enough to live what you discover in prayer.

September 9

At the end of the world you will receive a new body,
but you only get one soul. Take care of it.

September 10

You can drive down the wrong side of the road
but before long you'll get hit.

September 11

I was once asked, "What is the worst sin?"
This question opened a discussion in which all of the six people at the table involved themselves. I'd like to relay some
of the ideas that were shared so that we can reflect
on God's forgiveness, our lack of forgiveness, and
the injustice of sin in all its forms.
The first person spoke about murder and the next about rape.
The emotions of all ran high until finally I felt it necessary
to comment, especially as the question had originally
been asked of me.
I said, "If I committed an offense against God by telling a lie
and it was the only sin ever committed, Jesus would still have
come to earth and died on the cross just for that sin in order to
redeem me." The conversation changed. We stopped looking at
the sins of other people and began to examine ourselves.
We recognized our sinfulness. We appreciated that
the common ground we held was in our brokenness.
Meditate on the effects of sin. Your sin.

September 12

Practice some kind of fasting lest you become a slave
to your body.

September 13

You told me that you have a desire to grow spiritually.
If this is the case, pray, practice mortification, and examine
your conscience. Do each of these regularly.
There is no surer or more direct path to holiness.

September 14

All your relationships will improve if you don't judge others.

September 15

There is a constant battle being fought in my heart, and in
yours. The battle is between love and power, between the love
of power and the power of love. The more the power to love
grows within us the more our love of power decreases.

September 16

There will come a time, eventually, when you don't know
something. It's okay. It's nothing to be ashamed of.

September 17

Do not renounce the faith for a contemporary discovery in science.

September 18

Nobody can take your bath for you.

September 19

A very important element of wisdom is knowing when to act.

September 20

Give your life to God. It is the only thing He desires of you.

September 21

Have you fallen? In a large or a small matter? What matters is not what you have done, but what you will do. If you are humble you will beg forgiveness and try again. If you are proud and arrogant you will dig an eternal grave for yourself with more of the same mistakes.

September 22

Find me one time, event, or instance, when God has not been faithful to His promises. There are none. He will also be faithful in His promises to you. Our God is a God of faithfulness. Do not doubt His Word.

September 23

You have to take your feet off the ground to fly.

September 24

The desire of modern men and women to exclude God
from their lives is the ultimate contradiction of reality.
Without God you can do nothing.

September 25

Our inability to appropriately and adequately express our love
for the people in our lives is so common in an age
when communication is supposedly at its best.
Tell someone today how much you love and appreciate them.

September 26

Some things have little or no importance in relation
to the salvation of your soul. Avoid these things.

September 27

The smallest matter becomes great when disobedience
is involved.

September 28

The human touch has an incredible healing power.
Reach out to someone today and just hold their hand
or hold them in your arms and comfort them.

September 29

You live your life as if Christ had never come, as if you did not
have an immortal soul, as if there was no eternity.
It is no wonder you are unhappy. Nothing could be sadder.
Nothing could be more of a lie.

September 30

When you come to recognize and believe that you are a son or
a daughter of God you will also become aware that you lack
absolutely nothing.

October 1

When Satan reminds you of your past remind him of his future.

October 2

Don't project your sins onto others.

October 3

If you have the things of this world, but can do without the things of this world, then your heart will have the detachment that is necessary to make prudent and wise decisions.

October 4

Life is full of tough lessons. Learn them, don't resent them.

October 5

You know you have become a fool when you believe
you don't need to change.

October 6

You take too lightly what God expects from you and
are always trying to reduce it to a minimum.

October 7

God writes His own history books.

October 8

Seek out that gentleness within you that encourages people
to feel comfortable around you.

October 9

Most dreams only present themselves once in a lifetime.

October 10

People are always asking me for practical ways to adopt
the gospel message in their day-to-day lives. Here is one:
everything you see in me that you don't like or disagree with,
change these things in yourself.

October 11

Your mere presence should be a ministry.

October 12

God always rewards faith.

October 13

Jesus didn't come to condemn you; He came to save you.

October 14

Christianity is not an excuse for complacency and laziness.
Now that you are working for God you must work harder
than ever at everything you do.

October 15

One of the biggest mistakes you can make is to take yourself
too seriously. This leads to pride and pride to a fall.

October 16

No vase can overflow if you never fill it up.

October 17

If things are in a mess, accept that things are in a mess.
Everything doesn't have to be worked out right now.

October 18

You are called to be a leader and the only way to lead
is with an example of virtue.

October 19

I was pleased to hear that you visited Jerusalem, the Holy Land.
You have walked where Jesus walked, now walk as Jesus walked.

October 20

Don't belittle the things that are important to other people.

October 21

You asked, "What most needs to change in the world?"
The reply, "I do."

October 22

Today make one resolution — something you can do daily that
will help you to experience God more in your life. Live that
one resolution and you will experience a happiness
that will allow you to climb to new heights.

October 23

May God bless each one of us with prayerful spirits and
gentle hearts formed through prayer. God will use prayerful
spirits and gentle hearts as instruments to bring about unity.

October 24

When you share, your happiness expands.

October 25

Don't dialogue with the tempter.

October 26

Amidst the noise of the world you will find the highway
that leads to hell. In the silence of prayer you will find
the narrow trail leading to eternal life.

October 27

Pray for those you know who have died.

October 28

The only power Satan has he has been given by men.

October 29

If you want to improve your quality of life — pray.

---------→⊁ October 30 ⊱←---------

The productivity of the wicked often exceeds the productivity
of the righteous. They are working all around you hard and
selfishly. You must work at least twice as hard and selflessly.

---------→⊁ October 31 ⊱←---------

I thought I would never get through today.
Everything seemed to be on top of me. But I did and
I know there is a lesson to be learned.
When life gets tough break the days up into the smallest units
of time that you can. Then deal with them one by one.
Usually all you will have to deal with is the moment.
When you see it as it really is, you realize
that you can do it. You can do it.

November 1

You say to me, "I am only one person." This is true, but look at
what other great men and women before you have done in the
span of just one lifetime: Francis of Assisi, Paul,
Thomas Aquinas, John the Baptist, Augustine, Teresa of Avila,
Thomas More, Edmund Rice, Don Bosco, John Vianney,
Dominic, Patrick, Rita, Mary, and of course, Jesus.
Look also at what others have done in our time:
Mother Teresa, John Paul II.
They too could have used the excuse, "I am only one person."
The difference is they didn't see themselves as one person,
but rather as one part of one body. Then, dedicated to the
gospel message of Jesus Christ they chose to serve, and
to choose to serve is to choose to love.

November 2

You are not answerable for the first impulse.
You are for the second.

⊰ November 3 ⊱

Jesus said, "Love one another as I have loved you, it is by this that all men will know that you are my disciples." It is this love that gives us our identity as Christians. Have you lost your identity as a Christian in the middle of the world? Do you need to rediscover your identity as a Christian?

⊰ November 4 ⊱

You tell me that you are in love. If it is not the virtue of the other person that has attracted you then you must question your motives.

⊰ November 5 ⊱

I have seen people answer questions about the faith with incredible logic and inspiring wisdom. I think this gift is a result of: forethought, devotional prayer, philosophy, and theology. The world and the Church needs more men and women with this gift. If we can relieve the confusion, we will set humanity free.

November 6

Life is a pilgrimage, but sometimes you need a pilgrimage
to discover life.

November 7

You isolate yourself from people who challenge you to change
and grow and surround yourself with people who demand so
little of you. It is no wonder your progress is little if any.

November 8

When you come to meditative prayer always bring something
to read to help you overcome distractions.

November 9

Sin brings unhappiness.

In February of 1995 I visited Honduras which is located in the
Caribbean Sea. Leaving the group I walked through the streets
of poverty and disease wondering what life would be like
if I were to live there.

After purchasing something in a store I stood holding
my change and having a fragmented conversation with one
of the locals who only spoke a little English.

After five minutes or more the woman behind the counter
signalled to me to give back the change from my purchase
which I was still holding in my hand.

I hesitated for a few moments because I already thought she
had not given me enough of the foreign currency.

Finally, I handed her the change and after shuffling around
in her money box she handed me back some money —
more money than she had originally handed me.

I believe our experience of surrendering to God
has some similarities.

We are scared to abandon what we have and
give everything to God in case we end up with less
than we started with.

Fools we are! God always gives more
than what He asks from us.

November 11

The motto at my high school was, "LUCEAT LUX VESTRA," which is Latin for "LET YOUR LIGHT SHINE." On each day of my life to live this motto will be a new challenge.

November 12

Look at all the things you have that you don't need.

November 13

Small can triumph over big. It has before and will again. If things seem against you, hold your head up, persevere.

November 14

Today do someone an anonymous favor or send someone an anonymous gift.

November 15

To find truth you must be true.

November 16

If you are wrong, admit you are wrong.

November 17

In every moment of your life you make a decision for God
or against God. Every decision you make has a
supernatural value and effect that will last for eternity.

November 18

Fame and fortune are only illusions.

November 19

Everybody has a need to give.

November 20

This Christmas take as much time and care preparing
your soul to receive Jesus as you do to prepare food,
gifts, and, your clothes.

November 21

A man whose friendship has helped me greatly wrote this
grace before meals: Lord, we thank you for the food we have
and the friends we have. We ask you to bless and
console those that have neither. Amen.

November 22

Society is wrought by fear. Fear is the cause of so many problems, so much anxiety, and even illness. Could it be that there is a lack of love in the world?
Perfect love casts out fear. Could it be that there is a lack of love in your heart?

November 23

Time is a precious gift. It is so precious that God dispenses it to you one second at a time. Don't waste time.

November 24

Until you can learn to let someone else be in control you will never be in control, and you will never be happy.

November 25

It is in feeling loved that I am able to love.

November 26

God loves a cheerful giver but He also loves those
who are able to receive graciously and thankfully.

November 27

Until you can settle the war that is raging within you there will
never be peace on earth.

November 28

Invite someone occasionally to come to church with you.
Accept the fact that they may decline. If they do,
encourage them to go to whatever church they belong to.

November 29

Stop and listen to the music of a street performer.

I was walking in the shopping mall and I saw a young boy drop his treasure. It was a single penny. His mother pulled him along and said, "Don't worry about it, it's nothing." The young child didn't agree and he wept. I don't know what the lesson is in what I witnessed, but I know there was one. Maybe more.

December 1

You said to me, "Why are you always trying to change the world?" I replied, "Why aren't you always trying to change the world?"

December 2

Don't forget the poor.

December 3

Do you want to be great? Born in a stable...served all men...was criticized for His attempts to live and proclaim the truth...and He suffered.
He was the greatest.
If you want to be great, be little.

December 4

Sometimes you need to let yourself be hurt
rather than hurt someone else.

December 5

Next time you think things are not going well for you
visit a cemetery. Things could be a lot worse.
Take heart, look up, have faith, and rejoice in life.

December 6

Don't entertain false joys.

December 7

Over coffee a man said, "Our role as Christians is to serve.
Serving is not about ability, it is about availability."

---⊶ **December 8** ⊷---

You cannot become more like Christ and stay as you are.

---⊶ **December 9** ⊷---

You are saddened at the errors being taught. The only way to fight error is to proclaim the truth.

---⊶ **December 10** ⊷---

Behind every happening there is a providence.

---⊶ **December 11** ⊷---

Don't turn your back on those in need.

December 12

You asked, "How much should I give?" The reply,
"Give until it hurts."

December 13

"You are the salt of the earth" (Mt. 5:13). In the time of Christ
salt had two purposes. Salt was used to preserve meat
from corruption and to add flavor to food.
You are called to do the same in the world today. Through
your words, actions, and influence you are called to preserve
your family, your friendships, your workplace, and society from
corruption as best you can and to add flavor to these
environments by bringing Christ and His message to them.

December 14

Very often the only thing I learn in a day is that I cannot live
the wisdom I already know.

December 15

Prayer transforms everything we do into excellence.

December 16

Pray for unity among Christians.

December 17

Be patient in all things except in your zeal to bring
the Word of God to all men and women.

December 18

I believe the greatest of all human sufferings is to feel alone.
Visit someone this week who needs your company.
You will bring the light of Christ to that person's life and
you will learn more than you think.

December 19

Let go. It is the hardest thing to do.

December 20

"You are light for the world" (Mt. 5:14). While many around us are consumed with discussion about the prevailing darkness in the world, there is only one answer. Light.
Children of God are children of light. A torch to the world is what you must be. Not like the torches we use today that we flick on and off with a switch and batteries, but the torches they used in Christ's time. A piece of wood with some material wrapped around the top lit with a live flame.
Whatever that flame touches: your clothes, the furniture, curtains, carpet, will be set on fire.
When you become a torch set aflame with the love of Christ, wherever you go, whoever you meet, every person and every place that you come in contact with will be set on fire.

December 21

As Christmas draws near remember: Jesus is coming,
prepare the way.

December 22

Jesus washed His disciples feet. The Church needs to
learn to serve again. You need to learn to serve instead of
always wanting to be served.

December 23

Some things are important. But, no thing is more important
than anyone. For everyone is one of God's children.

December 24

Lord, I trust in your plans. Please show them to me.

December 25

You cannot become more like Christ and not become
more perfectly human.

December 26

Until life within the womb of a mother is safe,
life outside the womb will never be safe.

December 27

Human gospels don't solve problems. They don't work.
They don't help anything or anyone. You think by watering
something down you are helping the person. Stop giving
people your own gospel; give them the gospel of Jesus Christ.

December 28

To love less is never the answer. The answer is always
to love more.

❧ December 29 ❧

Your soul is like a garden. Sins are the weeds, virtues are the flowers, prayer is the water, and the sacraments the sunlight.

❧ December 30 ❧

Next time you pass a cemetery say a prayer for the souls of those who have been laid to rest there.

❧ December 31 ❧

Christ wants to reach out and touch every person on earth. He wants to extend the hand of love and friendship to all. The problem is very often the only hand He has to use is the one attached to the end of your arm.

About the Author

MATTHEW KELLY is a New York Times best-selling author of sixteen books, an internationally acclaimed speaker, and a business consultant to some of the world's largest and most admired companies. In Catholic circles he is perhaps best known for his book *Rediscover Catholicism,* which is the most read Catholic book of our times.

To learn more about his work, visit:
www.DynamicCatholic.com
www.FloydConsulting.com

THE DYNAMIC CATHOLIC INSTITUTE

[MISSION]

To re-energize the Catholic Church in America by developing world-class resources that inspire people to rediscover the genius of Catholicism.

[VISION]

To be the innovative leader in the New Evangelization helping Catholics and their parishes become the-best-version-of-themselves.

■■ DynamicCatholic.com
Be Bold. Be Catholic.®

The Dynamic Catholic Institute
2200 Arbor Tech Drive
Hebron, KY 41048
Phone: 859-980-7900
info@DynamicCatholic.com